Impeccable Regret

Also by Judith Fitzgerald

Poetry

Octave (1970)
City Park (1972)
Journal Entries (1975)
Victory (1975)
Lacerating Heartwood (1977)
Easy Over (1981)
Heart Attack[s] (1983)
Split/Levels (1983)
Beneath the Skin of Paradise: The Piaf Poems (1984)
The Syntax of Things (1984)
My Orange Gorange (1985)
Given Names: New and Selected Poems 1972–1985 (1985)
Whale Waddleby (1986)
Diary of Desire (1987)
Rapturous Chronicles (1991)
Ultimate Midnight (1992)
Habit of Blues: Rapturous Chronicles II (1992)
walkin' wounded (1993)
River (1995)
26 Ways Out of This World (1999)
Adagios Quartet:
   Iphigenia's Song, vol. 1 (2003)
   Orestes' Lament, vol. 2 (2004)
   Electra's Benison, vol. 3 (2006)
   O, Clytaemnestra!, vol. 4 (2007)

Biography

Building a Mystery: The Story of Sarah McLachlan and Lilith Fair (1997)
Sarah McLachlan: Building a Mystery (2000)
Marshall McLuhan: Wise Guy (2001)

Impeccable Regret

POEMS

. . .

Judith Fitzgerald

with an introduction by Thomas Dilworth

Talonbooks

Talonbooks
278 East First Avenue, Vancouver, British Columbia, Canada V5T 1A6
www.talonbooks.com

First printing: 2015

Typeset in PT Serif
Printed and bound in Canada on 100% post-consumer recycled paper

Interior and cover design by Typesmith
Cover painting by Alison Dilworth

Talonbooks gratefully acknowledges the financial support of the Canada Council for the Arts, the Government of Canada through the Canada Book Fund, and the Province of British Columbia through the British Columbia Arts Council and the Book Publishing Tax Credit.

LIBRARY AND ARCHIVES CANADA CATALOGUING IN PUBLICATION

Fitzgerald, Judith, author
        Impeccable regret / Judith Fitzgerald ;
introduction by Thomas Dilworth.

Poems.
ISBN 978-0-88922-949-5 (PBK.).

        I. Title.

PS8561 I88I46 2015   C811'.54   C2015-904158-9

To George Bowering, R. Bruce Elder, C. H. (Marty) Gervais,
Daphne Marlatt, Kerrigan McDonald, and Erin Mouré with Love

\

The feelings that hurt most, the emotions that sting most, are those that are absurd — The longing for impossible things, precisely because they are impossible; nostalgia for what never was; the desire for what could have been; regret over not being someone else; dissatisfaction with the world's existence. All these half-tones of the soul's consciousness create in us a painful greyscape, an eternal gloamstate of what we are.

—— FERNANDO PESSOA

But the dark pines of your mind dip deeper
And you are sinking, sinking, sleeper
In an elementary world;
There is something down there and you want it told.

— GWENDOLYN MACEWEN

Contents

Introduction

It is about ... how everything is a balls-up & a kind
of "Praise" at the same time.

— DAVID JONES

The value of literature is its beauty and truth. Truth in Judith
Fitzgerald's *Impeccable Regret* is triple: (1) loss of humanistic
culture to reductive, rationalist-materialist civilization;
(2) intensely felt private loss: broken love affairs, the death of
an only son for a father, the death of a friend by suicide. These
are analogous to cultural loss, all sharing "universal finality"
in what she calls "the grand scam of things." So "wake." This
word means (and all the poems together mean) what it does
in *Finnegans Wake*: "wake" up, realize your losses, undeny
them; "wake" or grieve them; and "wake" from the dead. The
latter metaphorically happens when — and this completes
her trinity of truth — (3) beauty (in art or nature) or love (in
relationships) transforms or compensates for loss. Beauty and
love imply an unspecified metaphysics that has its image in light.
But the poem "*Cogito Ergo Doleo*" mentions "my Friend" (with a
capital *F*) and "His blood, ruined body, love" as exemplifying such
transformation of personal calamity. The poems of powerfully
felt loss easter by appreciating and making beauty, "cryogenesis"
transforming suffering into celebration or praise.

The beauty of this poetry is, in turns and in combinations,
delicately exquisite, clunky, multivalent, polyphonic, port-
manteau, kenning, punning, colloquial, arcane, gently lyrical,
neologistic, allusive, and (pervasively) playful. Her puns and
neologisms are themselves mini poems: from one poem, "caligu-
lations," "regretitude," "neocoinjoinings" (the latter, alliances of
neocons devoted to money). This poetry extends the tradition
of rich poetic language flowering in Gerard Manley Hopkins and
Joyce in *Finnegans Wake*, rooted in Keats and Shakespeare. Like

Joyce, Fitzgerald sometimes sounds like Hopkins. "Whatsun, donesun . . . Smokebrick, . . . scumblight, / Stunsunk, stardark" — words from "Céilidh," a treasure of lovely, enlivening sound and varying-lovely rhythms, which evokes Hopkins because he was the first ecological poet and this poem concerns the eclipse of nature as "Forest fires smoke city air" in a "human blaze" that is global warming and more.

So these poems are modernist in immediate intrinsic form as well as message (cultural loss), though their extrinsic forms (lyric length, verse-lines, stanzas) are largely conventionally pre-modernist. Many of these poems retain for me unsolved mysteries, an aspect of their vitality, but rereading expands and deepens understanding. To comprehend most of them (you will, if like me, need to) read each one three times before moving on to the next — so that you can say with her, "we / did time / between / the lines." Why bother? Because so many of these poems are major. Let's look together at a few that establish larger cultural loss as context for personal losses.

In the poem "Deceptive Cadence," the Burning Lady (who allows Christopher Fry to remind us that *The Lady's Not for Burning*) is humanistic culture. You are addressed as "Fleeting Star," an allusion to Keats's "steadfast" "Bright Star" (ditto for "ShyStar" in an adjacent poem). Invited to "break out the world's tiniest violin," you are called to regret; and, with the poet, are implicated in the burning by identification with Nero, responsible for the burning of Rome — he is said to have played the lyre (which colloquially became "the fiddle") while Rome burned. The Lady is "A blazing building, bodies trapped inside," "Saint Stone" to rhyme with Joan of Arc. The humanity she contains is reduced by fire of materialist positivism to "nought but molecular carbon fraught with sparkglint / needles down-dark raining," exploding in heat or on pavement. This is 9/11. (A later poem in the collection refers to Conrad and Joyce as "Twins towering down scorn.") This calamity, the destruction of humane culture, prompts getting of "orchidectural clarity" (beauty of orchids and architecture) in "tonehall" (music, poetry) or in nature, where "melodious spurscores . . . smoulder, slashsigh, earthtrample, breakdamage, or downdapple" (hurray, Hopkins) "abalone string-fingering, wavelength clashing, clear cutting through your head." Cataclysm and art (Nero fiddling) seem to clash, as do death and beauty in nature. But they do not, since biology and aesthetics differ categorically. So calamity is and is not imaginatively redeemed by art as was (my examples) the Fall of Troy by Homeric epic, the fall of Celtic Britain by medieval romance, and the Decline of the West by literary modernism. Aesthetically (because of the human condition), nothing succeeds like failure.

"Phrases of Sorrow Conjure Wandering Stars," a gentle, lyrical call to "discover/Who goes among green visions utterly encharmed" to "Solve and Salve Life's Robulous Rebus" — its Möbius strip puzzle is, via Romulus and Remus (the Roman Cain and Abel), fratricide. The artist making myth out of suffering is a "Screamer-/Dreamer" attracted to natural beauty. (Fitzgerald is, like Keats, an incurable romantic — sorry, but Keats's early death is pertinent to all this.) The nursery game of life ends, "All fall doom"; but Fitzgerald enjoins the artist, "Rode hard, hastened harder. Love Lift in Light Attired." Here, even before noticing the allusion to Alexander MacLeod's beautiful collection of stories, *Light Lifting*, I got goosebumps.

The poem "No Signal Input" directly evokes the fall of the twin towers by quoting "You have/a new message" from Michael Symmons Roberts's great poem, "Last Words." Despite or because of "Babylonian loss," the always-new message is a call to love and build, to make art, here evoking the climax of the soliloquy at the end of Joyce's *Ulysses*. The response to the great "no" of physical calamity is moral/psychological/aesthetic "yes," the lover/artist being "true-/blue" (sad/faithful) "Penelope."

As you read through this book, you will notice that in the midst of civilizational darkness and personal loss, Fitzgerald celebrates cultural lights often by name, sometimes in barely noticeable hints — consider the wonderful concluding lines of "Breaking News" — by lightly punning on titles that recall David Jones and David Foster Wallace. She herself shines very bright and belongs among them.

— THOMAS DILWORTH

Impeccable Regret

DEAR READER

Hello, There . . . Howzit? I hear you — Been
Where, done what? Learned abso-deffo zen-zap-zip
Zero-zilcharoo until one appeared too near you?
We say Ixnay on the cloudspray, agency Earsay,
Regency light. G'Night, Mother Might, G'Night, G'Night.

Welcome, M'Dear 'n' Cherished Reader. Welcome
To Our New-World Ordered, flux-familiar bordered.
You will immediately recognize its utterly brazen
Shuddering attack-lack of down-and-dirty disguise.

O, lavish parade of freshly skin-skimmed foreign aid
Milked to the max: Sea roiling, his constangular boiling
Point . . . And all that which implies, impugns, repo ultra-
Glides comblastious. Ascension in bled-red lather. Pax.

Growing, glowing, going gone when it all goes hellarious?
O, Dear Snipper-Snapper, even Dearer Gripper-
Slapper Wonder-Whipper where every silver lining
Features a zipper. (Another day, another deficit.)
All Fall Down. Ol' Possum Rulez. Man in a Million, eh?

My Love, My Love, My Eternal Blaze of Brittle Glaze.
Grimpasse sur Mont Parnasse Tomb in plain abstrain
Anguish — Kiss her shapely sweet ass. Notoriocrass.
Valence versus High Holy Mass. Say, half a nice day.

> Full disclosure. Fracture bones. Skip stones.
> Why refuse your life, Jim-Jam Slim-Slam?
> Entreatly allow conspicuous consumption,
> Reinforce your murder vision, Hoardherder?

Grimslum, bloomstun, here comes exenocoluthon
Right on cue. Fasten your seatbolts. Travelling
Lodge Lander's End Game — Help your collocated self.

Or forgive this upstart heart's enshrined faith in dread art,
Its inverse on the impulsable mythereens crystalline
Undines; but, palpably present among skin-thin invisible
Defeat, utterly awestricken, thanks to Lady Brutalia Beat.

"O, didja say-saw, Jimmy, down at The Fist 'n' Pout?"
Still a pirate of extracurriculur circumnavigation.
Jumpstart your heart — Reset it to that yesterday
Just before you reconnoîtred illusionsway. Here, Dear

Reader: I freely share the key unlocking the eternal mystery
Yielding to your blue hue: *They Shoot Horses, Don't They?*
O, Terrora, O, Madre — Smother, Sister, Slaughter, Daughter;
And, you? Forget punishments wrought past due. (They do.)

DECEPTIVE CADENCE

To Nicholas and Karl "Rampike" Jirgens

Let's break out the world's tiniest violin, play the universe's saddest song,
and discover what you learned about freedom's glory. Shake and wake me
from this frozen slumber with technique to burn. Look at you, Fleeting Star.

The world ain't a ghetto. The Lady's Burning Man-Issuant name? Sublimity,
after the minim twinim mountain unto the flesh-singed chill of wise-ass byplay,
following catgut ecstasies scorched against her, short-circuited (maybe).

A blazing building, bodies trapped inside. She saw the clean, the sun flashing
open clasps on command for the last revolution, for the final conflagration,
Saint Stone. Hellions toss more fuel on the rock face of it, the rip-chase lit-hit.

"These corpses represent nought but molecular carbon fraught with sparkglint
needles down-dark raining." You hear those explosions on this darkling night
unvarnished? Then, you must search for orchidectural clarity in the tonehall.

Or find that cottage on the moor, locate those singular melodious spurscores
where they smoulder, slashsigh, earthtrample, breakdamage, or downdapple
abalone string-fingering, wavelength clashing, clear cutting through your head.

PHRASES OF SORROW
CONJURE WANDERING STARS

This hour. That exotic repose among flourishments
With a generous side of seductive sighs voiced (hold
mind daze). Emboldened. Gentle romp, pure lyricism.
Dove, fluttering and flivvering in the dark pine-wood
On a fishing expedition, a singular mission to discover
Who goes among green visions utterly encharmed,
In nightshell, O, swell, ShyStar, exposed unharmed.
Frail free. Lean out of any Window. Myth-maker

Sui generis: Solve and Salve Life's Robulous Rebus.
This NothingNoise seeks counsel or that hooded moon;
Unearth a mindful scrim of bright caps. Screamer-
Dreamer or incandescent streamer by twilight turning
To amethyst come-hither. All fall doom. O, the way
He demanded whether nobody understood at all there,
Scraping further. Elemental filamental strands of flim.
Rode hard, hastened harder. Love Lift in Light Attired.

NO SIGNAL INPUT

This viscous evening, its vulnerable liquidity? O, here, hold
these bones so close and hard against you, so crushed,
they break into your heart all over again. You have
a new message. Who does NOT? Yes, even
dew drips a name. Please, send flanges, O-
rings, coping saw, word, image, catalytic
flame (or reels of upstream drifters
swimming, glaze-glinting in these
swollen rivers of Infinitude
lapping those shores
of Babylonian loss before
you, righteously runned down
by drunk Taxicab of Absolute Reality)
because here — Hear? — Magnetic North?
No Eternity outside Time's Incarnate rifts exists
to play hide-and-hinge with cloud shudder and rogue
lightning pitched in Mind conjoining pulse of Remembrance
and you? You forgot, you blithely forgot. Why did you forget
torch-bearing scorch-daring the night his Dog smiled knowingly
acquiescing or agreeing or, O, that awful deep-down lashing Torrent
O — And the sea — the spreading sea crimson sometimes, crenelated
and that glorious yes, spun from the sun, sometimes, soft-settling
upon a red Yesterday signalling yes you will [or simply forget]
Independent Weekly Expositor forever barring or sinking
through next-best never's blip-zap gaps). Does true-
blue Penelope wait or end her lyric on the fickle
finger-pluckings of fate luring that shared ol'
bursted Moon, sometimes? New Loves
me loves you, [Tom] sometimes?

You had to be t/here (but, yes, you, Horizon John, rode radiantly).

INDEED

Sometimes, neither frequently nor often, she still soft envivifies

How his amazing son, his first-born prodigy and prodigal maestro
Unconditionally accepted his dictatorial leadership, his uttered
Insults, tumults, assaults, and bewildermentals so fucking far

Beyond comprehension; and she thinks, truly and fully thinks,
In this Age of Dread looming over all of us, she knows a secret
About a father and a son, the one he simply loved tomb much

And could lose him, could lose his right-hand man and get left
Stone-cold alone, in the frost etching the windows of houses
Where he would never cross the threshold, never meet another

Who became not only his most virtuous and irrecoverable player
But also his guiding light, his heartsake staked, in soothsayer
Dynamics. He loves him still, knows about molten love, hoards

That love and never shares it capaciously; but, that son, that star
Guided by the madnight moon, Mother of all Mothers, knowing
Completely and unspoken, so strong and unbroken, breakthrash.

Sancta Patientia! A lightdress gone. She was fluttered. *Nuée!*

EXISTENTUALITY ONE : SWOON OF SHAME

O, Sanglorians, habistacularly entwingled,
dibracious alltitudes (precisely pro-screwcue,
marchmalltitudes meltswelling, driftspelling,
morgasmic) forbiding, pastgliding, hearracane,
windownpained splinders, their too-blew tone?

O, Out amoung innumberustic lunarplexia:
Speak, Memoria, spinshine on the incline,
climb these concrete caligulations, sheerly
embraceletted and necklaced, shy glinces.

O, Metafaker, killer hurtbreaker, underslide
of overjoined, expaired, unpained, steering
the slip into its tagsloop, her slag-troopers
dwindlifying, gathersheered, embrickabracks,
chewsing the seenery, placid installations.

O, Seeradaude, inelucive, nothinges, creafted,
whipcode cracked, slyly emplanted, scapegrace,
nixed-to-numbthing, something you said, once,
holding my hungry exposture, sealerity, crushed.

O, Utterlantic, feelowing in your prantic dudsteps,
that luminant ruination, pathogentling, azaleazure,
nightsigh skyblastic, reclination, regretitude; but,
yes, those astonishing gardenial unions, evaporous
conjoinings, neocoinjoinings, the weddring works.

GRACE LANDING

Keeping a lo-pro, squeezing between crevices,
  seamlessly sidestepping hi-pri musical sirens . . . O, predators, parasitings,
    sociopathammrings, y'all self-destruct, camouflaged by darkness,
    swellead sharks. Blastbright viridescence, fluorescent seizure site
    amaze activated by wavelengths of visibly blue eminentalist poetics
    or experimential illumination situations, *significado obstinato*. O,
  recall yearn yawl? Upturn, downspurn, scorchburn? O, Fortuna : O, Lyra.

There, sheer irrefuturability of finitude building,
  this unparalleled heliotropic periwinkling glorioso play
  remains, encarved upon our frangible Coney killstrings
  in lonesome-on-her-ownsome anthemic disarray.

QUE BESA SUS PIES, QUE BESA SUS MANOS

The delicate gorgeosity of your vital words,
each shimmering with irresistible possibility,
barely containing the truth catching in one's throat,
such exquisite intensity, the blackness each repudiates,
porous with damage and longing, indelibly sorrow-
streaked in one transparent universe where knives
of knowledge carve wide swaths through history,
luminous among moon's slow-dawning curves, now
arcing to pull you towards the radiance of darkness
serrated, swallowing pain, gasping for clear sheer air
in those shadowed chambers of the heart yielding
to the contours of thinking skin in the perfect syntax
of stone and aether, grasping the universal finality
language's liquid purity salvages almost anything
but that, solves all conundra but that, that which
you cannot overcome, that cacophony of time wound up,
ground down, astounding in its irrefutable injury;
the circus of our love, its amusement-park attentions
spanning a millennium of, ultimately, swift midnights
(where the hands on the doomsway clock stand still
an instant, stand at attention, stand ready to embrace
whatever remains of a human face gone missing
without a trace). Hear that? It is cold; it is lethal;
and, it is threatening to break into itself in the name
of answers materializing on the horizon when the sun
rises to reveal dysphoria in all its splendorous glory.
That? Think crux. Think matter. Think father,
son, and wholly ghost-trace host. Think shatter.

HIS VIRTUE

Take, for instance,
this time, this place,
this window on the world
permanently blackened,
terminally intransigent,
palpably crackling
right down to the left.

You, sorry, for all of it,
for too many faces
donned in the flash
of mystery, full-frontal
easiness, uneasiness,
hectic tragic, myth magic
mirroring flesh of my flesh,
fallen, humming, "It Takes
Time" (and what else)?

You, I mean, you, no soul
bared, history harsh; always
so soft, sweet, slow, going
down by dawn's articulate light,
I do, though, mean, You. I do.

Somethere, something *is*,
winnoning, chiselling, revealing
crimson-shadowed cold-gleaming
streaks of lightning, ice-spiked.

POINTS ELSEWHERE

To X-IT Daniel Jalowica

He inclines his head towards midnight's guttering clashes,
acutely intuits his role in this exiguous tableau of ashes —
her pitched darkness, restively keyed to the art of damage
(or drama, tires screaming, the spectral careening glazing
her panic dread — automatic — smudge of violet swells
marrying vague horizons — her personal hell exposed —
his hand held just so, hers shielding face from lips to lashes).
O, God, he loves her. He's sorry. He's a fucking monster.

She reaches out to someone who cannot hear nor help her
because the roar of the ocean swallows voices and cries
with astonishing swiftness, with supreme disinterest
in all-too-familiar re-enactments of primeval mortiferous
brutalities beyond comprehension — Chrysanthemums?
Christ, recall all those wild Irish roses brambling hair
and skin, their bloodless petals sharply carmine and brilliant
in their absolute faith beauty's future remains secure?

It gathers in its arms ice-rough raindrops pooling beneath
blankened sky, its articulated layers unfolding dusk-deep colour
fastening stem to starblight, predominantly xanthous gangrene,
now, indigo-mauve broken. The ocean a ghost mirror in denial
roaring its growling stamina — its inexorably seductive pull
embattling the only way out — out of the question — the only
way back to healing, leaving love alone to fend for its besieged
self in the bruised rainbow of bituminous rage-blasted eye.

SHE HANDS
THE KEY TO YOU

Józef Teodor Konrad Korzeniowski;
Or, James Augustine Aloysius Joyce?

"The horror! The horror!"
The UK. The Congo.

Now, when you enter
Heart of Darkness

You exit knowing
The former coming;

Testament torn; rivets
Twins towering down scorn.

The latter going.
Rad-Trad flowing.

You see ash, only ash
Gripping islands miraged.

ONE NATION BEYOND FIXATION STATION

To John Doyle (with gratitude / in celebration)

An incomprehensibly shattered tale commences
In medias res for our contemporary Shakespeare
Reinvents Hamlet bypassing specious superfluity
And egregiously revengious fallen angels loosed
Upon the living and the dread-stricken deadbeats
Of esurience (for reasons weary we cannot see).

With every character ghostguarded and mirthless
Just north of LA / CA, with faintly menacing
Landscapes reassuringly familiar, you look
At this stale, desiccated place and understand
Bereft inevitably equals grifted malnourishment
Or, given its surface-glistering evidence, *faux* grace.

You descend that spiral stair where, once there,
Each step reverberates with sheer certainty, nothing
Can rescue you from the glare of mirrorsheen,
From an aggravated assault endured to come clean,
Admission or commission, all fall folded, con-
Strutting, struck shutting down serous grid zero.

RETICULATED SALVATION

Splendid cowboy Boots on the ground, Coney sound.
Bow to your Partner; Far Rockaway three sheets
To the wound [down] demanding Soul admission
Or attrition; O, some kind of response on Prime-

Time Dime, no lesson, only wheels up
After hitting the Tarmac; O, soar, Seer,
OverSeer, floor it. Man in the muddle:
Flanked securely by Him and Holy Her.

You intuitively knew how one Deciphers
The cosmic telegraphics, moving targets,
Perceptions cruelistically empheral, yourn-
Consequent Desire, vivid dream overseen.

Cellophantasm: Nettled DanMa rah-rah rattling
Hysterianna, Damn Ya! You remain. Welcome
To some twenty-cursed century, the one where Dis /
Ease manipulates and Heart-warn *la-ti-da* madaminates.

[SOMETHING, THERE IS, THAT DOESN'T LOVE A WAIL]

To Stan Rogal with Love

You smash-ravished your way
off that drizzirriguous Holocaustic mountain
of Shoah skulls, wound boundup; then, wound down
with a virtuosic-effectuated view consummately full of right-
for-picking regrets. You gets, gives, goes, or rogaluess. (Still. She shout: Yes.)

CÉILIDH

BY SUSAN MCMASTER AND JUDITH FITZGERALD

Forest fires smoke city air charred
Crabtree leaves kick
And scutter side-on to early sun —

Whatsun, donesun, smudged care
Holding down the heart against onslaught
When caught in the muddle of what?

Everything we believed and all that
Faith given over to truth we began to learn
The past, deceived but not deciphered

Nor intuitively strummed by the Lilliputian
Orchestra of morning — despite darkness —
Glory sundark, devoured, even country air

With hemlock, cedar, and barricade now gone
Sunsunk, starblight, thinking thinking stun —
But, no, that never yielded a path in smoke

Nor evening glow, alive and living, giving
Too much but never enough, human,
O, so human touch till finger on fiddle strokes

The between aether, ion, or sparkladen haze
With hairstrung bow, arc, and blow of whistle,
Harp, jangling guitar stomping out the beat,
Shoulder-to-shoulder, knee-to-knee in firelit

Smokebrick, chambered hum, and scumblight,
Stunsunk, stardark yield to this human blaze —
Universally incoherent — that "natural" raze.

BEREFT

We don't know when
You left — when you
Left us to die.

The truth, always
Slippery — bows,
Exits stage depth.

Look! — Agony!
Silvered cobalt —
Ventral plastron —

All illusion —
Ary, self-absorbed —
All guilt — all gone

Missing with maw
Gaping, aping
That brutish gaze.

TRAIN OF THOUGHT

To Beep with Love

Gone there [plot]

   Seen that [fraught]

     caught the long [forgot]

    shot [nought]

      not terminally bought [slot]

       O, Saint [distraught]

        that's all she [wrought]

He could not fail to cross that [spot]

Nor cannot blot surgeon's knot [dot]

TO THE BOSS

He taught me
To say
I need you.

TRIANGULAR BENEDICTIONS

To Leo Mon Amio

He also taught me, O, things you learn from intuitive adoration
and you know they matter because spans later, the medals
and goblets, glittering, untarnished, stand at the ready
and it's a swing and a miss and a swing and a hit
and she's going going backwhack gone
coming all the way home with sleeveheart and soulglow
while a halo of binding love enfolds and no one strikes out
since hosts never disappear, simply burn brightly, ignite lightly
or rightly, poetic justice held so impossibly gently ache dissolves.

SHE WILL MOVE THE WORLD

To Dana Randall

She did love you, once; she heartfully believed
your seductions, ablutions, and castigations
until she did not love you, after that night
you fastened her to obdurately howlerious
hallucinations, believing her gone enough
not to petition the suffocantic bigger bluff . . .

What you strictly wanted, patently, patiently,
involved eyes closed, legs open, slight hands
frozen at the fulcrum of the cracked black ice
at dread centre of your supra-unblemished heart;
incapable of feeling, happily preferring to fuck
that big brain into quiescent mediated oblivion . . .

Knowing she would continue to knock you
into your crowded schedule of fresh flesh;
abandoning percipient purity, exact otherness
or selfless need, you settled for distractions
on death row in that hospitalized prison you,
My Love, with cruel calculation, constructed . . .

Expressly intricate for those shadow women
who soon came to know you would not go
beyond that sick bay of veridical querulosity;
O, you turned sadistics into straps, republics
of forgiveness chronically desecrated, acutely
implacable. Talk fragile truth: Triage no option.

SACRIFICE

it goes wonkily circular, some move
meant to placate imagined shibboleths
since none exists, not really (or, more
to the point), not any longer

you want a hand
worth holding, you need stability
beyond that band
standing in for humility

does arrogance ever turn against itself
or do these representative specimens
take hold and hang so hard, so heeling
you feel the serrations, sharpened, teeth

you want, you want
so much in your utter denial
of every ounce of humanity
transporting, inevitably, elevating pride

for you; you wander all too tidily
among the relics and remonstrations
containing the chaos of history
leaving this planet (then heading home)

WELL. HELLO. THERE.

                    Did you see
                 those barbs
            launched
at someone
           too close
                 to read
                    the riot act?
                       Me, neither.
                 S'Okay.
His explicit
   blade creates
            a shroud
                 on the back
                       of what
we agree
            to call
                 civilization.
                       Hello? O,
                 wake. (How
            in the hell
did vivarious
            she break
                    into me?)
                 Well, deeply?
Your place
                 in single file
                       evaporates.

                 There. This
            will find flesh
acumangled
            in tenebrously
                 bound splinkers.
                          Don't delay.
                 Now. Today.
            Or accept
            this reception
created
            [cremated]
                 exclusively
                       for, well . . .
                          Someone
                 [somenone]
            knows who.

NIGHT-STEPPING IN THE KEY OF C

1

Your song
before
all gone
stun wrong
cruising
the I-
nine-five
watching
Key West's
sharpened
focus
knowing
heart-broke.

Lounge scene,
lushly green,
palms lean
into rhythms
of where
you swear
you never
went; no, can-
not explain Me
Drames sent.

You cross
slightline
sightlines,
spare this,
share bliss.

Nightly
lightly
stepping,
hearing
Lucille
before
you see
him play
and know
that song,
all right
all wrong,
you turn
off, turn
down, turn
up, turn
over your
inner-station
calibration.

2

Did you see
something
that never
happened
to doomster
in lunacy's
loquacity
before she
took a name
in vain?

"We can't do
without twins."

(Upsomdowns
Ebbrous Coinci-
Dancer Cancer.)

Nevermind:
O, nevermind.

She breaks
into tears
recalling stories
of velvet night
strokes holding
happy-go-gusty
notes a fraction
beyond right
royal excursions
into hallowed
half-steps
too holy
to never let go.

COGITO ERGO DOLEO

Who lives in the wing not visible,
Squarely opposite you, sad Voyeur
Of the Visceral? Think Velázquez.

Think signal-to-noose ratio. I, too,
Grateful, fateful. My Friend, it flows
Freely: His blood, ruined body, love.

EXISTENTUALITY TWO : WAVE
OF RADIANT SILENCE

How I wanted you, hearthening, soulstitious,
wholly opensighed, seaswirl ingathering, leaving
your damned wreck, my tearstream, interramingling,
celebreathing, neither burning nor brimmingling;
simply falling off the nearest horizon to discover
another integument, puissant, O, so elegant
carresting, wantonwound tight dragright down
to the forgiving archfigure (salvocation, sluice,
sinduction), spinnydipping by indistraddling,
commangling (read: intermixual fusespoke,
combustiously one). Still, alive with language
coursing through crafty-grifter you know who;
we concede decorously: Live outrageously.

Not an important failure, manifestations
simply a quiet all-consuming conflagration;
our world exploding in hush of flamelight,
in territorial moonlight's wispsere swathes.
It matters. It doesn't. Arsy-varsy. Full stop.

What comes next? A delicate balance
nix-to-nothing, nought-to-nothingness.
What I wanted. What you held aloft.
Sonder prison a punishment. You think
I don't know you by now? Thought not.

Lonely, so lonely, crushed under its weight
this glimmering evening, so close to twilimn
perfection in the ultimate freedom, no signal
input, no signal-to-noise ratio, no integrated
circus about to materialize in silicon *Nibbāna*.

WE HIT OUR BVM KNEES / SASHAY SWAY

The entire sensorium synchromeshin' in tandem?
They don' like our type 'round here, don'tcha know?
Right. Night and day. A joyous sadness, one holds
Another sacred and never lets them go, even when
They're gone forever. Secularly sacred, not Christ,
Not th'udder guy . . . Adds another angle on "It hurts
So good." Catharsis always does. 'Course, I grew
With my tiny-burden way. A swakeeper. You made
Your bed; now, you can danned-well die in it.

In the meantime (which grows increasingly
Small-madded and cheezily-meazily meaner),
Do enjoy this day as happily and divinely fine as —
Almost all of — You always make pacific mine:
TransAtlantic frantic prantics/Knocketty knock . . .
"Who's there? War wages where? Whose war?
Did we win? Hiss shooter? Can we expect more?"
Nein, Fräulein. Status quota. Below the lowest:
Knock, knock. I R . . . Whither thou goest . . .

The thing, here lies the thing some call "elephantom":
Divorced from furniture, dart fulsome bulls hit on toast.

FOR THE RECORD

She knows hoardheart you, now, in the only way
You need knowing. What's in knowledge, oddly,
something comparable with fair wisdom, evenly.

A noun. A verb. A breath of shared history.
Framed in pale matte-made light, sun underside,
your figure wrought — caught between enter or exist.

Remember how she gently pushed greed-needy you
back to your first true calling — collect — always?
How, muses she, did you so slyly keep it all (under control)?

Eyes on the prize, one you knew would never own you;
on the wrecks for the bitter, this one takes the ache;
you still cast backward glances, in dawning nightplots.

First: Untangle the hopeless thoughts holding you
aloft for too many years — then, upon departure, proprances,
withhold goodbye — selfishness eclipses sky's burner cry.

As you were. Stand down. Give up self-sufferance
for the span left to you in this harshly unforgiving
landscrape. (*Hush, Mama.*) We know you'll never return.

So little ever mattered to fascinating me-me-meistic you;
buried alive; still, unconscionably forcing her to survive
with neither love nor listening — S'Long gone missing.

DO U KNOW Y?

Swinglow, St. Stolen-from-Us
(When that cold collaborative light
In the ultimate theatre went blank.)

Depression, anger turned against the self extinguished,
Teaches what history never will: Pig. Trough. Patience
Is a victory in the grand scam of things (conspicuously).

Not U, no. U, M'Dearly Missed Darlin' St. Deep, would never
Mourn one arrow world, could never pick clean carrion shadows
Cast by a moon carved twentieth-century maudlin : *EM TY*.

STILL HERE

Perhaps you believed solitude
exactly the opposite of all of that,
whatever that reveals. Face facts:

Your televisual version of this world,
the one inhabited by pyschotic home
movies redeemed by exuberant crises.

The ground floor. Ahead of the times.
What good could a .303 accomplish?
Did Uncle Amos ever wake from coma?

The fascination still alive for criminals
allowing Jo McNo or Dan The Man
the opportunity to variously revile

or admire (or, astonishingly) both.
Time to stop falling into your world
ill-equipped to turn back her hands.

[Perhaps not.]

LOVE LETTERS

You want to hold fast & fasten,
hold fastened to drowned rings,
to make sense of anachronistic
sodalities' directions, keygrippt
under full-frontal revelations
locked in family-ranked stations,
situations & naked nations,
            snipset or tripdebt (fair game):
            scrambling, brambling for shame.
    Soul far, snapset, trapdebt, in-
        déniablement. Tosst did she,
wedding band sinking slowly
in the definitive happy ending
featuring you with she, mother
            plus eldest boy all blacksheep
            for to target too easily asleep,
            for all in the book of eternity:
            Ah, no matter (even though
            she stealth-steadily slithered
            quietly into your show, sprawl
            crawled, renegade, good goal).
            Stripped you of Leo's lovely lies,
            of Arc A's precious studhorse alibis.

SONG

Revelling in the grovel
Writhing with the grief
Claim-staked bejesus hovel
Upended beyond belief

She opened your faultless letter
She almost found the heart to read it
Somehow, someday, when sentences sound better
She may ache enough, she may actually need it

A slow-smoulder fire glows indigo felicitous
Lacking nothing, she goes into the dirt
Hair entangling with roots of azalea
Her, following a dull gauze moon, hunter-full, hurt

HAMLET WITHOUT A HEART

In the grand scream of all things true,
It never really made a difference
What strangers gave of exactly you
(When it came to host-trace ghost).

Beyond shielded fade-grey hues
Window on one blackened world
Where all such unpacked blues
Wound up in ground-down squalor.

O, never the fault of that foul father,
His sign, this heart-cracking thrust:
L'évocation aveugle de la tragédie
Builds eviscerations: Rust-red dust.

MERCY, AND YOU?

Ah, there . . . You keep leaning into that raw future
With your feet fleeting . . . fleeing; or, perhaps
I see these leaps too clearly? Not a good plan.
Plan B-Day on D-Day *boom-chuck-a-boom* sway;
But when you work the line, you play it, too . . .
Then, everything depends on what-the-fuck reflections;
Clusters of elegantly strung words smoothed by you:
A crimson star on the horizon, electrically palpable,
Transplendently rich, open so wholly, resplendently so hue.

PHOENIX

"I'm burning up the road
I'm heading down to Phoenix..."
— LC, "I CAN'T FORGET," I'M YOUR MAN

You know the road to hell
too well to believe pavement
could survive that blast, ash
phalt always, a word you know
but could never spell, would
think ash fault and wonder:
How in the hell does that factor
into the general view of anything?

Well, hell. An endless con-
struction site, really. You told
her over the long weekend: "We
shall all become CanAmericans; I
shouldered that truth; and, hell
froze over." Always telegraphic,
an orange crush, red tide, blue moon
brought low by Lord knows who.

ONCE
IN A BLUE MOON

To Dorothy Mahoney, Karen P. Ouellette, Paul Vasey, Lenore Langs,
C. H. (Marty) Gervais, and Marie (Pottle) Groundwater with Love

Leila Pepper leaves us
A legacy of enduring and formidable depth
and strength, of sisterly knowledge, of breadth —
She leaves us
The heart of the better part writ large
On that tablet we call the soul —
And, soul she remains, her indefatigable spirit
Flourishing moment by moment from this now
To the next and next. O, we know, we know
Leila did not die, she stepped gracefully into eximious.

REVENIR À MOI

Don't.
Forget me.
Don't.
Forget we
did time
between
the lines
we could not
eradicate,
everything
we knew
far too well:
thin scars,
Dog Stars,
what remains
intimately
exhausted
in this life
of remains
gone to hell.

ALTOGETHER ELSEWHERE

O! Wither'd is the garland of the war,
The soldier's pole is fall'n; young boys and girls
Are level now with men; the odds is gone,
And there is nothing left remarkable
Beneath the visiting moon.
— ANTONY AND CLEOPATRA

Altogether elsewhere, out there, a star-crazed mirror
Affords a brilliantly fractured panoramic view of truly you
Mourning, inborn, brought to your hands and needs
To importune onsettling paramnesia — dying, dying —

Now, you face chaos, tracing shades blasted and blue
Before scabrous retrospection cracks open the winter
In your eyes, fails to conceal the unreal you never reveal:
Those shreds of self buried alive; that ego's consuming drive.

A wire recall of spokes; monstrous turnings of the machine.
Hindsight sepulchres past fast time reeling in the backstory,
Rasping, grasping for the ended hour of sequestered clarity,
You suppress all in secret service to your thin edge of glory.

SCIO ME NIHIL SCIRE

Your infallibility and obvious gentility
Place you in that race through poetic space:
Forward, one more bloodied robin, skinsloughed.

HOLDING PATTERN

When now became unbearably halituous then
unendurably blessed, when clouds overhead
opened their eyes upon this wretched stretch
of history, when the prisoner stood at the gate
and begged admittance to escape that fate
worse than hate-bait, harder than forever, O,
your scent filled this air brittle with supple
and disciplined suffering, the garden reeling
among wheeling galaxies and again you see
these edged rows, that river's scars, striations,
and wounds only you could inflict *tabula rasa.*

a garden. a future. a warden. a culture.

Hoc autem scito, quod in novissimis
diebus instabunt tempora periculosa.

REVELATORY IRRUPTIONS
DANS L'ESPRIT DU TERRORISME

Peeling veil, mask, persona, personalization, personification,
dazzling brightness, and necrotic abyss; sky rolled up, a scroll
drawn back, a curtain; there's a joke, clown, whited polyandrium,
dollop of quicksilver, scudding rubescent and violet clouds falling
from hysterical sky, smell of history and thorns, blood roaring
in ears, calloused hands encarving moistly mangled heart incarnadine;
a poet, a trickster, a punched line, the futility of communication
corrupting signal to news in electric avowa where matter rises
from the virtual foam of quantum universes, where emptiness
equals full balance, where you wonder who I am but fail to ask
yourself the same question. Why ask me? Look inward, Stranger.
Your angel already left home. You have all the time in the world.

COSMIC EMPATHY

To R. Bruce Elder with Love

She thinks of fracturable you almost departing
                              for the duration
                   And reminds herself ranges
                              of mist-shrouded mountains
Yield to spang-swirling breezesways. Looks up : Takes small
              Comfort in absolute certainty
                         the finest minds [Delphinus/Upsilon Scorpii/Aquila?]
                              secure Apodis
To Vulpeculae, multitudes,
                         serried, glowheart circularities,
                   cincturing streak-glittering across the canvas
                              of infinite connection.

ELEGY FOR AYANNA BLACK

We shall miss
her presence
in our shrinking
world forever;
yet, somehow,
we shall feel
her among us
always (ever).

In the name
of Father,
of Mother,
of Sister Poetry.

BLOOD CULTURE

In Memoriam Robert Kroetsch
(26 June 1927 – 21 June 2011)

BY LEONARD COHEN AND JUDITH FITZGERALD

Night comes quietly when you discover the simplest
of light lifting its wings to block the carnage.

How do you manage these broken days?
Can you believe what happened with the riotous?

You knew something got lost in the translation
so you stole that language, that lexicon, the only life

Capable of proving none exists except as converts
to some thing or other, lists magnificent or mundane,

Knew what lay in waiting for those western stars fading
against the unforgiving intrusion of what happens

When comets or catastrophes ricochet above the screech —
Or, do we mean roaring? — All nor nothing, just like that.

Amen.

26 June 2011

THE END OF THE LINE

To Gwendolyn MacEwen with Love

Driving home, braving that Hemlock Road exit,
Sunblind with rain clearing away shred detritus
Of too many years of grief. Passing Rye Road,
McFadden Line, Saint Mary's Catholic Church,
Thinking some little life writ large on past pages
Matters or makes any difference to anyone else.
The Old Scribblers, how they suffused that dying
With calm ecstasy and dignity, finessing the truth
On these hurtblast roadsways. Hemlock : Carnage.

SIC TRANSIT GLORIA MUNDI

To Robin Blaser with Love

A crumpled flag flies at half-mast today
In the recesses of our sadly shattered heart,
For one of our original's gone his own quiet way;
Canada's irreplaceable one's a soaring world apart.

The jittery robin on my lawn skip-tentatively sings;
Soon-to-be-lilacs on thin trees promise-speak joy;
But let us recall life's fertile forest and fecund things –
So much more than ideas for Robin Blaser,
                    our ageless boy . . .

EXISTENTUALITY THREE : ACHE OF LOVE

And, yes, you will, heartpouring,
love's image, fond yet too far,
scandalously bearing longing
proud and fallen, forbidden,
stilled, pressing, ill-darkened
in that unquiet ceaselessness
where she waits, too touched
to believe, too gone to grieve.

[IF NOT, WHY NOT?]

If not, why not winter, why not
telegraphic orthonymaniacal
exquiescence? (Because

smugly wrought exultant counterfrightful thought gloss
embraced a label until the thrust beneath, now a genius,

pulled the wail over readerly suspension
of protracted grief, cryogenesis, disbelief,
closed the book on the eternal axis of inscrutability, folded
on the straight-lashed cast of minions proffering irrefutability,
shattered in the notion regarding the depths of regret,
concerning wholly and fully starting again), got it, want it & still . . .
to [. . .] get.

IMPECCABLE REGRET

O, give us this day our daily dearth;
My Friend, My Darling of Catastrophe
Enticing the moon, efficiently learning,
Slowly turning away from the gruesome
Spectacle, slyly fading, failing sightline,
Exiting through common-ground down;
But, should you reconsider, unsunder
Every lie-for-lie truth sadly laid bare
On those ivory keys: Play "Goodbye";
Discover how long you long for the past.

. . .

Your sorrow flows into a Renaissance sea
    of certainty;
        and still, now, her vibrant final words to me,
      paradoxic, the preparations complete,
       depression lifted, work. Now,
    it brings me to my knees, that she shot
        her brains out, splatter-shout.
I love her, I cannot love her, those long-distance
                  nights we sliced open history
till silence spoke eloquently? Sandra, you promised.
    Then? You left us impoverished.
   In that space of shattered sorrow
  that never fills us up again,
       so distant,
       so far gone beyond
  tears it breaks every bone
       in my ravaged savaged heart
         demolished all over again.
     Crumbled. Crumpled. Shred.
     Torn. Bound. Tethered.

                  O, Unforgettable You?
                  Now among your angels
                  holiest on high, mother-
                  of-pearling aether, takes
                  one, the arch marching
                  orders, makes one, ashes
                  scattered across the bay,
                  breaks one, O, open so
                  broken. Love, I look away.

. . .

All right, okay. I accept the impossible since
there's nothing times nothing here left to lose
no matter what parts of exigent angeltecture,
guttural or grievous, you refuse to choose, ever-
mending, neverending, stain of heinous bruise
spread swirling, downbroke, wrong-way cruise.

YO AHORA ESTOY DELGADO
Y TU AMORE ES EMMENSO

The truly innocent yet lucent urgency of love
Stays with me, always an alluring green light
Before the Bedamned Man hauls right off
And smashes Ol' Ek's specs, willing blindness
Or chilling kindness. So, let's get down to brass
Facts, really: Once a sociopath, always
A spectator at the main event, consumed
With blank holes at the centre of embuggerance,
Beating against the current, burying IT . . .
(Those Albemarle days now appreciated;
One plus one equals criss-crossed two.)

CONTEMPTUS MUNDI

He unfolds and smooths your annotated life starry;
no matter, no mindfulness, even less indifference
past imaginable. Talk invincible defeat. Go ahead.
See if I cry. Life worthy of affirmation, glimpses
of discovery, delight, a thrilling quietude prevails.

. . .

Still, you go down
that cragsteep slope
for his reassurance,
if deep nothing else.

Dew-lined,
sun-blotted,
dust-crusted . . .
Adieu, adieu,
you do not
visibly fear
the welt-
beaten path
where he
let loose
and you
counted
horseshoes
on your arse
you survived
harsh blows,
harsher hooks,
too hurt-broke
to see the way
he absconded,
terminally gone,
wholly ensaturated
with the soured milk
of human kindness.

BREAKING NEWS . . .

. . . Maximum security prison escapees may have had help.
You think? Mental exploration of the logic driving criminally
insane during the execution of another human strain. *¡Ay,
Caramba!* (Here, one humiliated *howler* locates The Sea
of Tranquility, blocks out foundation, unearths intermolecular
configurations highblighting the many ways to smash a life on the rocks.)

. . .

Of course, of curse, we, the chorus of impeccable regret,
barely audible, nakedly verbal, miscible, a nix-mix line down-
and-disorderly shape and meaning above and beyond the call
of beauty, so very confused even refuge evaporates, intertwingles,
conjoins with battersmasher, bitterhurter, fearhunter, *et so forthia.*

Comfort takes cover under sadness (in the grand scram of give-
and-fake). Look, your hard-hearted heroes rise in eerie unison
to plan an elegant legerdemain. Ingression, parading raw egos
ripe for redemption. Break the rules, create the crush of all of it,
yesterdead. Take your time, My Guide, My Guardian, My Grief.

At some atomic level — O, Chevalier — a garden, a garland
once removed from jests both infinite and inviolable, gawd-
damned nightmares populated with sere ghosts. *FinnWake.*

MISSING

We settle for what settles for us, after all that passion and anger,
after learning the perfect alphabet of the heart by the light
of too many black nights of the soul, the ones where you rush
into battle only to prove, yet again, not your mettle, no;
only to prove the art of fiction, myth, and fabrication your domain.

It will never matter to you, never matter one iota more
than this evening tumbling across, rumbling across, stumbling
into dusk gone AWOL. You decreed your need to punish
everything never mattering, anyway. It takes two takes
to do a double, to overlay prey on the predator gone astray.

SHATTERING

Yet do I fear thy nature,
It is too full o' th' milk of human kindness
To catch the nearest way.

— MACBETH

All the words, expressions, and remonstrations
cast in the past which *n'existe pas*, how could you
fail to support the one pillar of strength who got you
when she caught you, tore you away from intimacy,
not quite your speciality, if she recalls anything
about you at all. Just some shadow drifting farther
into the universe, long past the aurora borealis,
the twins, the milk of human kindness even Lady
Macbeth considered part of an essential arsenal.

SHATTERED

You know, let's go, let's outrageously flow
Into the mythstical, the slo-mo frame-by-flame
So-no glow . . . Emanulation, evacuumation,
O, welcome to our wonky world where E
= EmSee Scared with flags unfurled;
O, we bow, we scrape, we flash
On the drunken terror of that GG rape.

Did EL-O-EL-A ever consider no one deserves
A life-scar of catastrophe? We always attack
Ourselves first, My Friend, never an enemy.
Choose your targets with heart and learn
Love ain't blind (and hate ain't real, eh?).
Talk projection, the fake flake of labels.

Why hurt a woman when you built your life
Upon exactly that? GG? Peel the labels,
Dear Lost. Push down the lonesome, tear away,
And take a page from The Book of Eternity:
If not for this gift, it would dissolve; but, now
We both know the demons, sadly, so belong to you.

DRAMATIS PERSONAE : ENDERS WAY

Mind over mutter, bloodied entanglements.
Matter? Mater . . . She blew into our lives,
Flew, actually, an adumbral vulture, soot-
Blackheart, break-battered, end-splittered.

Once a witch, always a bitchuman, mean
And calculating, shockeen, fly-sky screen
Where you cannae please the queen o' Bs;
And, her mindnight wingspite crushplanned.

1
HOPENESS
[TROUBLE CLEF]

Cobalt, licksalt, weapon concealed, halt revealed
In the way she grasped our souls and laughed
At her branding, cruel landing, swoop disbanding
Until even we could see we would never be free.

ShamSheen. Mama hot-damn huzzah buzzardah
Because you cannot believe twins join to deceive
And language sours anguish, slideride exemplified
Up, down, cup, crown. O, broken knight, foul flight.

2
HOPENESS
[TROUBLE CLEFT]

You insufflated cauterized skin, rust, dirt, pin-thin;
Desesperanza, predestinación y gloria. The name;
Its echo fell across an explosive sadness floating,
The sweet river lifting her veil, coyly revealing aurae
Too true to express, too expressive to randomly hit
Bottom, riverbedding, runnerskedding, greendreading,
This brand, this marked skin forever encarved blue
With the massive damage only you intimately knew.
Dumb-down, splendid cowboy boots on the ground. Singular
sound, digging up bones, echoes pushing down the lonely.

> ". . . marked a place . . . on my skin
> need navigate . . . with his name
> he sunk so shone
> I ain't never . . . bin the same . . ."

TRINITY

To Fiona Kinsella, Paul Lisson, and Vesna Trkulja-Stevens with Love

You walk across the floor of my brain and your light floods my veins,
You whom I have never met (yet to whom I feel so close, even when
You are not here in any tangible way, shape, frame); you still remain:
Palpable, phosphorescent, casually, on a hard high road, shoring up
A woman, revealing the impeccably correct route, the side glide never
Glaring, calmly sharing such comfort, such fixed confidence. You lead
Me into protective certainty, teach me to step so easily, momentously,
Into our parallel journey effortlessly. My Friend, how did you undertake
To unbreak memory, unmake history, reawake the righteousness of it,
The stilled centre of trust and faith yielding to it, always understanding
The sure knowledge no answer comes easily; but, that dreadfast panic
Quieted in the clear eloquence of connection, revelation, all creation?

. . .

Here comes energy-zappers, parasites, hangers-on, predators,
Danja-hysterics, bruises heart-shaped, the wearisome works.
Our lion severed nothing worth catalisping among use-ruse dues.
The way a world cannot exist despite love or golders-green excuse.
When we knew what proved Him real, what legitimately mattered?
Then we slow-dawning hoped all our delusions nose-dived shattered.
O, Love, we never replaced the joy we shared that glorious night;
But, the miraculous keeps us strong, prepared for consuming light.

. . .

Acknowledgements

I am genuinely humbled and deeply grateful to the following individuals for their support, encouragement, understanding, and editorial acumen (among innumerous blessings varia during this eight-year poetry seizure):

Adam & Martin Levin • Aimee, Caroline, Kelly, Tracy & Alan Norton • Ann-Marie Metten • Anthony Rota • Arlene & John (Smitty) Smith • Arnstein Garagiers Abby, Aimee, Ben, Donnie, Jeff, Magnum & Terry • Audrey & Sydney Davis • Blair & Patti • Bonnie & Doug Gorham • Brenda Leblond & The GrrLs • Butch Woolger • Chloë Filson • Christy & Karl Siegler • Clifford Hummel • Cris Cuddy • Darlene Nordstrom • Dave, Emily & Pat Lull • David Eso • David Gavan Baxter • David McCabe • David Staines • David & ValGal Cranham • Denise Tremblay Fownes • Dianne & Michael Czura • Dionne Brand • Donna & C. H. (Marty) Gervais • Dwight Yoakam • Eija, Jarkko & Rauli Arjatsalo • Ellen, David, Laura, Steve, Isaac, Ronan, David, Dick & Lenore Langs • Ellie Tesher • Eric McLuhan & E-CoHearts • Erin Mouré • Fiona Kinsella & Paul Lisson • Fiona Watson & Avrum Fenson • Garry Thomas Morse • George Elliott Clarke • George Maroosis • Georgia Nicols • Gerald Owen • Goddess Helen Floros • Hardwarriors Penny, Judy & Steve • Helen, Marcie & Michelle (of Huntsville's Hometown Pharmacy) • Gord Young (of *TNBN*) • Gracie, Harmony, Kelleran & Lauren Holman • Gregory Gibson • Guardians Marilyn, Norm, Scott & Val • HannaH GrrL • Heather, Courtney & Alexis Gysel • Jack Kirchhoff • Jason Blake • Jason Darling • Jean Baird & George Bowering • Jeff &

Duchesne Electriciana • Jesse Kohl • Jim & Louise LaPointe • John Donlan & Miriam Clavir • John Doyle • John & Lisa Kloberdanz • Johan & Karin Bosker • Judie, Jesse & Christopher Booth • Judy & Ted Pringle • Karen Jacobson • Karen, Trish, Tanya, Kim, Mervin, Casey, Lacey, Darlene & Albert (of Port Loring's Buchanan's) • Karl & Nicholas Jirgens • Kerrigan McDonald • Kevin Williams • Kitty Lewis • Lady & Lord Conrad Black • Leah Toth • Leo & Familio • Leo (Steve) Bloom • Les Smith, Jenn Murray & Rolf Maurer • Linda Leith • Linda Löwe • Lisa Way • LuDawg • Marina Warner • Mark, Destin & Lyric Lotton • Mary Beard • Mary Morea • Maxine Gadd • Maxine Whitehead • Mc • Mike McCoy • Mr. & Mrs. Brad Foreshew • Mrs. & Mr. Jack Tennant • Musia Schwartz • Nafeesa & Ziad Fazel • North Bay Airport Animal Hospitaliers • Ole Irenæus Wierød • Patti Garlic, Mitch Belanger, Vicki Tyler, Adam Contant, Richard Coffin, Brian Floyd, Nancy Slater & Greg Williams (of North Bay's World-Class Rock, *THE FOX*) • Philip Milito • rabidsenses • Rhonda Bailey • Rick Curry (Port Loring Realtor Extraordinaire) • Robert Kory (of Kory & Rice LLP) • Robert K. Schwartz (of Gardiner Roberts LLP) • Robin Robertson • Rus Bowden • Ruthann & Tom Dellandria • Rob Carrick • Sally, Marie, Michelle & Tom (of Necessities) • Sarah Jarvis • Sheena Branigan • Sir Peter Stothard • Smaro Kamboureli • Stan Rogal • Stephen Goldwasser • Steve Bennet • Suniti Namjoshi • Susan, Kim, Terri, Karen & Keon Nia • Susan Holbrook • Susan McMaster • TD & Zacharay • The Duchess, Chris, Jason, Matt & Pope Paul Ipolito • Tony Power • Valerie Shertzman • Victor Coleman • Vinay Menon • Wade Ferrel • Wesley Burton • Weyman Chan • Zoey & Alison Dilworth (for the felicitously perfect cover painting). *Vous êtes tous resplendissante.*

Without life- and vocation-saving financial assistance from Access Copyright, James Davies & The George Woodcock Fund of the Writers' Trust Foundation Committee, ODSP, OW, the Public Lending Right Commission, and the Ontario Arts Council's Writers' Reservists (Black Moss, Brick Books, Guernica, *Hamilton Arts & Letters*), *Impeccable Regret* would not exist. Thank you.

Earlier drafts of many of these poems and sequences first appeared in *Books, Inq.*: *The Epilogue, Chortler, Dusie, Cosmoetica,* Cranberry Tree Press's *Six of One, Hamilton Arts & Letters, Monsters & Critics, Poegles, Rampike, The Globe and Mail*, and *Wompherence.*

Requiescat in pace: Esther Cohen, Alistair MacLeod, Sandra Merriman, Leon Schwartz, and Peter Stevens.

Thomas Dilworth

Thomas Dilworth is a University of Windsor Killam Fellow and a Fellow of the Royal Society of Canada who specializes in Modern Literature and Romantic Poetry. He is the author of multiple volumes of literary criticism, one of which, *The Shape of Meaning in the Poetry of David Jones*, won the British Council Prize in the Humanities.

Judith Fitzgerald

Marshall McLuhan's official biographer, Judith Fitzgerald, is the author of twenty-plus collections of poetry as well as three bestselling volumes of creative non-fiction, *Marshall McLuhan: Wise Guy* (Dundurn, 2001) and *Sarah McLachlan: Building a Mystery* (Quarry, 2000) among them. *Rapturous Chronicles* (Mercury, 1991) was nominated for the Governor General's Award for Poetry while her epyllion, *River* (ECW, 1995), was shortlisted for the Trillium Award. The Poetry Fellow of the Chalmers Art Foundation's collection of ghazals and sonnets, *26 Ways Out of This World* (Oberon Press, 1999), was named one of the six best poetry collections of the year published in English (*The Globe and Mail*'s Top 100); additionally, *The Globe and Mail* again designated her completed Quartet one of its 100 best 2007 English-poetry works. *Given Names: New and Selected Poems* (Black Moss Press, 1985) was shortlisted for the Pat Lowther Award and earned a Writers' Choice Award. A senior contributing literary reviewer for The *Globe and Mail* (where she earned the Fiona Mee Award for her "outstanding contribution to English-language literary journalism"), Fitzgerald remarked, during a 2003 interview conducted by Jesse Kohl, "I do what I have to do in order to do what I want to do. Poetry is my vocation; journalism is my avocation. I create the latter to make a living, the former to make a life."